contents

THE CARIBBEAN IN A GLASS…

The drinks of the Caribbean are already well known around the world – there are few international cocktail bars without a favourite recipe for piña colada, daiquiri or Cuba libre. But other Caribbean favourites, such as the unusual stout punch, have remained an island secret. As with all Caribbean recipes, the key to success lies with the use of fresh ingredients where possible.

piña colada

1 cup (250ml) coconut cream
1 cup (250ml) rum (dark or white)
1½ cups (375ml) pineapple juice
1 cup crushed ice
1 lime, sliced thinly

1 Blend coconut cream, rum and juice in a blender or cocktail shaker about 30 seconds.
2 Add ice; blend or shake 30 seconds.
3 Serve in tall glasses, with a slice of lime to garnish.

serves 4

cream stout punch

Cream stout punch is a Caribbean classic. The ingredients are certainly unusual, but it can be curiously refreshing on a tropical day.

400g tin condensed milk
400g tin evaporated milk
1 teaspoon vanilla essence
½ cup (100g) light brown sugar
½ cup (125ml) white rum
600ml stout

1 Beat condensed milk, evaporated milk, vanilla, sugar and rum in large bowl with electric mixer until combined.
2 Pour milk mixture into large jug; add stout, stir well.
3 Refrigerate punch at least 1 hour. Serve in tumblers.

serves 4

left to right: cream stout punch; piña colada

pineapple orange frappé

1 medium pineapple (1.25kg), coarsely chopped
½ cup (125ml) orange juice
3 cups crushed ice
1 tablespoon finely grated orange rind

1 Blend pineapple and juice, in batches, until smooth.
2 Pour into large jug with crushed ice and rind; stir to combine.
Serve immediately.

makes 1 litre (4 cups)

watermelon refresher

900g watermelon, deseeded
   and coarsely chopped
125ml orange juice, chilled
40ml lime juice

1 Blend or process ingredients
until smooth.
2 Garnish with lime slices.

makes 1 litre

tip You will need a 1.5kg piece
of watermelon for this recipe.

virgin sea breeze

500ml cranberry juice, chilled
500ml ruby red grapefruit juice,
   chilled
40ml lime juice

1 Place ingredients in large jug;
stir to combine.

makes 1 litre

fruit daiquiri

1 lime
1 cup (250ml) dark rum
1 tablespoon dark brown sugar
½ cup (125ml) lime juice
½ cup (125ml) pineapple juice
3 passionfruit
¼ teaspoon Angostura bitters
2 cups crushed ice

1 Peel lime, avoiding bitter white pith; reserve rind.
2 Combine rum, sugar, juices, passionfruit pulp, bitters and ice in cocktail shaker; shake briefly or until combined.
3 Serve in cocktail glasses, decorated with a little reserved rind.

serves 4

carib champagne

1 tablespoon curaçao
2 cups (500ml) chilled champagne
1 tablespoon dark rum
1 cup (250ml) chilled pineapple
    juice

1 Combine ingredients in large jug.
2 Serve in champagne glasses.

serves 4

fruit punch

1¼ cups (310ml) fresh orange juice
1¼ cups (310ml) grapefruit juice
1¼ cups (310ml) pineapple juice
1¼ cups (310ml) ginger ale
½ cup (125ml) lime syrup
¼ teaspoon Angostura bitters
2 cups ice cubes
4 fresh mint leaves
1 lime, sliced thinly

1 Combine juices, ginger ale, syrup, bitters and ice in large jug.
2 Serve in tall glasses, decorated with mint and slices of lime.

serves 4

left to right: carib champagne;
fruit daiquiri; fruit punch

STARTERS & SOUPS

Most of the traditional starters on the following pages can be served either hot or cold. Caribbean soup can be anything from a light and delicious cold starter to a hearty meal of fish, meat or vegetables. We have given some basic recipes for traditional soups,most of which can be varied to suit your taste – so feel free to add any suitable ingredients that take your fancy.

chilli crab-filled peppers

preparation time 20 minutes
cooking time 5 minutes

3 large green peppers (1kg)
3 cups (510g) cooked crab meat
4 hard-boiled eggs, chopped finely
2 small fresh red chillies, deseeded, chopped finely
2 tablespoons finely chopped spring onions
1 tablespoon finely chopped fresh flat-leaf parsley
2 teaspoons finely grated lemon rind
⅓ cup (80ml) lemon juice
1 cup (300g) mayonnaise
½ cup (140g) plain yogurt

1 Halve peppers lengthways, remove seeds and membranes. Place pepper halves in large saucepan of cold water, bring to a boil; simmer gently, uncovered, 2 minutes. Drain peppers, rinse immediately in cold water; pat dry with paper towel.
2 Combine crab, egg, chilli, onion, parsley, rind, juice, mayonnaise and yogurt in large bowl.
3 To serve, spoon crab mixture into pepper halves.

serves 6

tip This dish can give out just a hint of chilli from the red chillies, or be turned into a really fiery starter with the addition of 1 tablespoon of chilli sauce.

coconut prawns

preparation time 25 minutes (plus marinating time)
cooking time 4 minutes

16 uncooked jumbo prawns (800g)
2 tablespoons lime juice
1 tablespoon dry white wine
4 cloves garlic, crushed
½ teaspoon salt
¼ teaspoon freshly ground black pepper
1 cup (90g) desiccated coconut
2 tablespoons finely chopped fresh coriander leaves
2 tablespoons plain flour
2 eggs, beaten lightly
vegetable oil, for deep-frying
2 limes, cut into wedges

1 Shell and devein prawns, leaving tails intact.
2 Combine juice, wine, garlic, salt and pepper in medium
bowl, add prawns; stir to coat prawns in marinade. Cover;
refrigerate 1 hour.
3 Combine coconut and coriander in medium shallow dish.
4 Remove prawns from marinade, pat dry with paper towel;
discard marinade. Place flour in strong plastic bag, add prawns
to bag; shake to coat. Remove prawns; shake off excess flour.
Dip prawns in egg, then roll in coconut mixture until coated all
over; press on coconut.
5 Heat oil in large saucepan; deep-fry prawns, in batches, about
1 minute or until golden brown.
6 Serve hot with lime wedges.

serves 4

escovitch

Escovitch was originally Portuguese, but is now found in dozens of variations around the Caribbean islands. This is one of the most popular versions. You can serve it on individual plates, but most people prefer to put the whole serving dish in the centre of the table and allow their guests to make their selection with toothpicks.

preparation time 25 minutes
cooking time 25 minutes (plus cooling time)

2 medium onions (300g), sliced thinly
2 cloves garlic, sliced thinly
2 medium carrots (240g), cut into 1cm slices
1 medium green pepper (200g), cut into 1cm pieces
1 bouquet garni
½ cup (125ml) white wine vinegar
2 tablespoons olive oil
12 green peppercorns
1 teaspoon salt
1 cup (250ml) cold water
500g red snapper fillets

1 Place onion, garlic, carrot, pepper, bouquet garni, vinegar, 1 tablespoon of the oil, peppercorns, salt and the water in large saucepan. Bring to a boil; simmer gently, uncovered, 15 minutes.
2 Heat remaining oil in large frying pan; cook fish, in batches, 3 minutes on each side or until golden. Place fish on serving plate; cut fillets into bite-size pieces.
3 Remove bouquet garni from pan, discard. Pour vegetable mixture over fish; allow to cool before serving.

serves 4

green pea soup

preparation time 20 minutes
cooking time 40 minutes

50g butter
3 shallots, chopped finely
1 medium sweet potato (400g),
    cut into 1cm pieces
1 medium red pepper (200g),
    chopped finely
2 medium tomatoes (380g), peeled,
    deseeded, chopped finely
2 cups (500ml) chicken stock
3 cups (370g) frozen peas
1¼ cups (210g) chopped cooked
    chicken
½ cup (125ml) single cream
2 tablespoons finely chopped mint

1 Melt butter in medium saucepan, add shallot; cook until shallot is soft. Add potato and pepper; cook, stirring, 1 minute. Add tomato; cook, stirring, 1 minute.
2 Add stock and peas, bring to a boil; simmer, uncovered, 20 minutes. The potato and peas should become mushy, but not lose their shape.
3 Add chicken; simmer, uncovered, 5 minutes. Stir in cream; simmer until soup is heated through – do not boil.
4 If desired, add a little salt and freshly ground black pepper. Serve soup sprinkled with mint.

serves 4

cream of coconut and banana soup

preparation time 15 minutes
cooking time 35 minutes

4 medium green bananas (740g)
2 tablespoons olive oil
1 medium onion (150g),
   chopped coarsely
1 clove garlic, crushed
2 cups (500ml) chicken stock
1 cup (250ml) coconut milk

tip This soup is also delicious served cold. To serve cold, allow the soup to cool to room temperature after cooking, then refrigerate for at least 1 hour.

1 Preheat oven to moderate.
2 Place whole bananas on oven tray; bake in moderate oven 25 minutes or until cooked. Remove and discard skins; reserve bananas.
3 Heat oil in medium saucepan; cook onion and garlic until onion is soft.
4 Add stock and coconut milk, bring to a boil; simmer gently, covered, 5 minutes.
5 Blend or process stock mixture and bananas until pureed. Return mixture to same pan; simmer until soup is heated through.
6 Serve soup topped with coriander leaves, if desired.

serves 4

fish and sweet potato chowder

preparation time 15 minutes
cooking time 40 minutes

1 tablespoon olive oil
1 small onion (80g), chopped coarsely
1 medium sweet potato (400g), cut into 2cm pieces
1 medium carrot (120g), chopped coarsely
1.5 litres (6 cups) fish stock
200g firm white fish fillets, cut into 2cm pieces
1 teaspoon finely chopped fresh oregano
½ teaspoon freshly grated oregano
½ cup (125ml) single cream

1 Heat oil in medium saucepan, add onion; cook until onion is soft. Add sweet potato and carrot; cook, stirring, 2 minutes.
2 Add stock, bring to a boil; simmer gently, covered, 20 minutes or until sweet potato is cooked.
3 Blend or process stock and vegetables until smooth.
4 Return mixture to same pan; add fish, oregano and nutmeg. Bring to a boil; simmer, covered, 5 minutes or until fish is cooked.
5 Stir in cream; simmer gently, stirring, until soup is heated through – do not boil.
6 Serve chowder topped with coriander leaves, if desired.

serves 4

tip You can substitute ½ teaspoon dried oregano for the fresh oregano.

CHICKEN

There are as many chicken dishes in the Caribbean as there are cooks.
These recipes show how Caribbean cooks have taken inspiration from different
cooking styles and given them their unique tropical twist.

sweet chicken stew

preparation time 25 minutes
(plus marinating time)
cooking time 1 hour

1 medium onion (150g), chopped
    finely
3 medium tomatoes (470g),
    chopped finely
1 trimmed stick celery (75g),
    chopped finely
1 tablespoon finely chopped
    spring onion
3 tablespoons finely chopped fresh
    flat-leaf parsley
2 cloves garlic, crushed
1 teaspoon fresh thyme leaves
1 tablespoon lime juice
2 tablespoons sweet chilli sauce
½ teaspoon salt
½ teaspoon freshly ground black
    pepper
8 skinless chicken drumsticks (1.2kg)
2 tablespoons olive oil
2 tablespoons dark brown sugar
2 cups (500ml) chicken stock
1 tablespoon tomato paste
2 medium carrots (240g), cut into
    1cm slices
1 lime, cut into wedges

1 Combine onion, tomato, celery, spring onion, parsley, garlic, thyme, juice, sauce, salt and pepper in large bowl. Add chicken drumsticks, mix well to coat, cover; refrigerate overnight.
2 Heat oil in large saucepan, add sugar; cook until mixture begins to bubble. Drain chicken; reserve marinade. Cook chicken, in batches, rolling it in sugar mixture, until browned all over and coated in sugar mixture.
3 Add stock to same pan; stir to combine stock and pan juices. Add tomato paste and reserved marinade, stir. Add chicken and carrot; simmer, covered, 45 minutes or until chicken is cooked through, turning chicken at least once during cooking.
4 Remove lid from pan, bring to a boil; simmer, uncovered, until liquid has reduced by about half, taking care not to let the contents burn or stick to the bottom of the pan.
5 Serve with wedges of lime.

serves 4

tip The key to this recipe is the caramel coating given to the chicken when it is browned in the oil and sugar mixture.

devilled chicken

preparation time 15 minutes
cooking time 55 minutes

30g butter
1 large onion (200g), chopped finely
2 cloves garlic, crushed
2 tablespoons tomato sauce
1 tablespoon worcestershire sauce
1 tablespoon French mustard
2 tablespoons mango chutney
½ teaspoon ground allspice
½ teaspoon salt
½ teaspoon freshly ground black pepper
8 chicken thighs (1.8kg)

1 Melt butter in medium saucepan, add onion and garlic;
cook until onion is soft.
2 Add sauces, mustard, chutney, allspice, salt and pepper,
stir well; simmer, covered, 5 minutes.
3 Preheat oven to moderate.
4 Place chicken, skin-side up, in oiled baking dish; pour sauce
mixture over top, completely covering chicken with mixture.
5 Bake chicken, uncovered, in moderate oven 45 minutes,
occasionally basting with chicken juices.
6 Serve with a tomato and chickpea salad, if desired.

serves 4

caribbean chicken hotpot

preparation time 20 minutes
cooking time 50 minutes

2 tablespoons plain flour
1 teaspoon salt
½ teaspoon freshly ground black
    pepper
8 chicken thighs (1.8kg), skinned,
    boned, cut into bite-size pieces
2 tablespoons olive oil
1 large onion (200g), chopped finely
2 cloves garlic, crushed
1 small sweet potato (250g), cut
    into 2cm pieces
2 medium carrots (240g), sliced
2 trimmed sticks celery (150g),
    chopped finely
2 medium green bananas (400g),
    peeled, sliced
¼ cup (50g) red lentils
1.5 litres (6 cups) chicken stock
1 teaspoon chilli sauce
1 bouquet garni
150g pasta (see tip)

1 Combine flour, half of the salt and half of the pepper in shallow dish. Toss chicken in flour, shake off excess.
2 Heat oil in large saucepan; cook chicken, in batches, about 5 minutes or until brown all over. Set aside.
3 Add onion and garlic to same pan; cook until onion is soft. Add potato, carrot and celery; cook, stirring, 2 minutes or until vegetables are lightly coated with oil.
4 Add banana, lentils, chicken, stock, remaining salt and pepper, chilli sauce and bouquet garni; bring to a boil, stirring. Reduce heat; simmer gently, covered, 15 minutes.
5 Add pasta; bring to a boil, stirring. Simmer, covered, 10 minutes. Remove and discard bouquet garni.
6 Serve hotpot sprinkled with fresh parsley, if desired.

serves 4

tips Penne, macaroni or shell pasta are all suitable for this recipe. This hearty dish is definitely a main meal! Our recipe uses chicken, but you can vary the dish by using lamb or beef, or even leaving meat out altogether. Stretch the hotpot by adding more stock. Or make it even more filling by adding other vegetables of your choice.

tobago chicken hotpot

preparation time 20 minutes
cooking time 1 hour

75g butter
1 chicken (1.5kg), cut into eight pieces
2 medium onions (300g), sliced finely
2 cloves garlic, sliced finely
1 tablespoon curry powder
1 fresh red chilli, deseeded, chopped finely
½ teaspoon saffron threads
1 cup (250ml) coconut milk
½ teaspoon salt
2 cups (500ml) water, approximately

1 Melt butter in large flameproof baking dish; cook chicken, in batches, 5 minutes or until golden brown all over. Set aside.
2 In same dish, cook onion and garlic until onion is soft and just beginning to brown. Add curry powder, chilli and saffron; cook, stirring, 1 minute.
3 Return chicken to dish, add half of the coconut milk, salt and just enough cold water to cover chicken pieces; bring to a boil. Reduce heat; simmer, covered, 40 minutes. Add remaining coconut milk; cook until heated through.

serves 4

tip Tobago chicken hotpot is traditionally served with plain boiled rice and side dishes such as sliced banana, chopped tomato, chopped red onion and plain yogurt.

jerk chicken

Traditional Caribbean jerk dishes began with dried meat, usually beef (or jerky, as it was known to sailors). In the days before refrigeration, meats – especially beef and venison – were cut into strips and dried in the sun to preserve them for long sea voyages. The meat was none too appetising at meal time, so the sailors made it more palatable by adding plenty of powerful spices. Now jerk dishes are no longer associated with dried meat, but instead refer to the fiery seasonings that give them their special flavour.

preparation time 15 minutes
(plus marinating time)
cooking time 55 minutes

2 tablespoons plain yogurt
1 tablespoon chilli sauce
1 teaspoon finely grated lime rind
2 tablespoons lime juice
1 teaspoon ground allspice
½ teaspoon salt
½ teaspoon freshly ground black
   pepper
1 medium onion (150g), chopped
   coarsely
2 cloves garlic, chopped coarsely
1 tablespoon grated fresh ginger
1 tablespoon coarsely chopped
   fresh coriander leaves
1 tablespoon wholegrain mustard
2 tablespoons light brown sugar
1 tablespoon olive oil
4 chicken breast fillets (700g)

1 Blend or process yogurt, sauce, rind, juice, allspice, salt, pepper, brown onion, garlic, ginger, coriander, mustard, sugar and oil until smooth. Place marinade in baking dish. Add chicken, mix well to coat, cover; refrigerate 1 hour.
2 Preheat oven to moderate.
3 Bake chicken, uncovered, in moderate oven 50 minutes, turning at least once.
4 Remove chicken from oven, place under hot grill; cook about 2 minutes each side or until browned.

serves 4

tip This dish can also be cooked on a barbecue or under the grill. For grilling or barbecuing, use a little extra oil in the marinade.

chicken with chickpeas and rice

preparation time 15 minutes
cooking time 40 minutes

50g butter
8 chicken drumsticks (1.2kg)
1 medium onion (150g), chopped finely
2 cloves garlic, sliced finely
1 fresh red chilli, deseeded, chopped finely
1 medium red pepper (200g), cut into 1.5cm pieces
1 cup (200g) white long-grain rice
2 tablespoons desiccated coconut
1¼ cups (310ml) coconut milk
1 tablespoon fresh thyme leaves
400g can chickpeas, drained
½ teaspoon saffron threads
2 cups (500ml) chicken stock
1 tablespoon finely chopped spring onions
1 lemon, cut into wedges

1 Melt butter in large heavy-based frying pan or paella pan. Add chicken; cook 5 minutes or until chicken is browned all over.
2 Add brown onion, garlic, chilli and pepper to pan; cook until onion is soft. Add rice; cook 2 minutes, stirring constantly, until rice is coated in butter. Add coconut, coconut milk, thyme and chickpeas, stirring well.
3 Stir saffron into stock; add half of the liquid to pan. Bring to a boil, reduce heat; simmer gently, uncovered, 20 minutes or until rice is cooked, adding more stock, a little at a time, as rice absorbs liquid. If you run out of stock, add a little water.
4 Serve topped with spring onion and lemon wedges.

serves 4

MEAT

West Indian cooks generally concentrate on lamb and pork, though goat is also popular. Beef dishes are more common in Cuba and the other Hispanic islands of the Caribbean. The meat dishes we have chosen reflect the wide variety of cooking styles and ingredients used by Caribbean cooks.

cuban char-grilled lamb with onion and pepper

preparation time 15 minutes (plus marinating time)
cooking time 30 minutes

4 tablespoons finely chopped fresh flat-leaf parsley
1 tablespoon sweet paprika
4 cloves garlic, crushed
1 teaspoon salt
¼ cup (60ml) olive oil
8 lamb loin chops (1kg)
2 medium red onions (340g), sliced thinly
2 medium green peppers (400g), cut into 1cm strips
1 medium yellow pepper (200g), cut into 1cm strips
2 tablespoons dry white wine

1 Blend or process parsley, paprika, garlic, salt and 1 tablespoon of the oil until mixture forms a paste. Spread paste over lamb until coated, cover; refrigerate 1 hour.
2 Heat remaining oil in large saucepan; cook onion, stirring, until soft. Add peppers; cook 2 minutes.
3 Add wine, cover; simmer gently, stirring occasionally, 20 minutes.
4 Meanwhile, cook lamb under grill (or on barbecue) until cooked through.
5 Serve lamb with onion and peppers, accompanied by mashed sweet potato and a green salad, if desired.

serves 4

lamb and lentil curry

preparation time 25 minutes
cooking time 1 hour 15 minutes

1 tablespoon plain flour
1 tablespoon curry powder
¼ teaspoon chilli powder
1 teaspoon ground ginger
½ teaspoon salt
½ teaspoon freshly ground black pepper
50g butter
1kg trimmed diced lamb
1 large onion (200g), chopped coarsely
2 cloves garlic, crushed
1 medium red pepper (200g), deseeded, cut into 1cm squares
400g can tomatoes, chopped coarsely
2 cups (500ml) lamb stock
1¼ cup (250g) brown lentils, rinsed and drained
½ cup (125ml) coconut milk

1 Combine flour, powders, ginger, salt and black pepper in small bowl.
2 Melt butter in large heavy-based saucepan; cook lamb, in batches, until browned all over. Set aside.
3 Add onion, garlic and pepper to same pan; cook until onion is soft and just beginning to brown. Add curry mixture, stir well; cook, stirring, 1 minute.
4 Add undrained tomatoes and stock, stir well. Add lamb, lentils and coconut milk; simmer gently, covered, stirring occasionally, 1 hour or until lamb and lentils are cooked.

serves 4

tip This dish can be served with plain boiled rice or on its own. Place bowls of mango chutney, chopped banana, chopped tomato, desiccated coconut and plain yogurt on the table as extra accompaniments.

spiced lamb chops

preparation time 10 minutes
(plus marinating time)
cooking time 50 minutes

1¼ cups (310ml) orange juice
2 tablespoons aniseed, crushed
1 teaspoon garam masala
1 fresh red chilli, deseeded,
   chopped finely
1 tablespoon honey
½ teaspoon salt
2 tablespoons dark rum
8 thickly cut lamb loin chops
   (1.4kg)

1 Combine juice, aniseed, garam masala, chilli, honey, salt and rum in baking dish. Add lamb; turn to coat with marinade. Cover; refrigerate for at least 1 hour, turning once.
2 Preheat oven to moderate.
3 Roast lamb, uncovered, in moderate oven 45 minutes, basting frequently. Remove lamb from dish; set aside in warm place.
4 Pour marinade into small saucepan, bring to a boil; boil, uncovered, until sauce has reduced by about half.
5 Pour sauce over lamb to serve.
6 Seve with a cucumber and mint salad.

serves 4

jerk pork chops

preparation time 15 minutes
(plus marinating time)
cooking time 20 minutes

2 fresh red chillies, deseeded,
   chopped finely
2 teaspoons finely grated
   lime rind
⅓ cup (80ml) lime juice
1 teaspoon ground cinnamon
1 teaspoon ground nutmeg
2 tablespoons ground allspice
1 tablespoon chilli sauce
2 cloves garlic, crushed
4 pork loin chops (800g)

1 Combine chillies, rind, juice, spices,
sauce and garlic in small bowl; mix well.
Spread mixture over both sides of chops,
adding a little olive oil to mixture if it is too
dry to spread. Cover; refrigerate 1 hour
or overnight.
2 Cook chops on barbecue (or under
grill) 10 minutes each side or until cooked
through. Serve with grilled slices of lime,
if desired.

serves 4

tip This jerk paste can be used with
other meats, such as lamb.

char-grilled pork chops with herbs

preparation time 15 minutes
cooking time 16 minutes

1 tablespoon coarsely chopped fresh rosemary
2 teaspoons fresh thyme leaves
2 tablespoons coarsely chopped fresh flat-leaf parsley
3 cloves garlic
½ teaspoon salt
½ teaspoon freshly ground black pepper
2 tablespoons olive oil
4 pork loin chops (800g)

1 Blend or process herbs, garlic, salt, pepper and oil until ingredients are well chopped and mixed.
2 Spread half of the herb mixture evenly on one side of the chops. Place chops, herbed-side down, under grill (or on barbecue); cook 8 minutes. Spread remaining herb mixture evenly on chops, turn chops; cook 8 minutes.
3 Serve with a mango or other fruit salsa, if desired.

serves 4

tip If grilling the chops, cook them herbed-side up so that the herbed side faces the heat.

creole pork

preparation time 30 minutes
cooking time 1 hour 20 minutes

2 medium aubergines (600g)
coarse cooking salt
2 tablespoons olive oil
1kg pork fillet, cut into 2cm cubes
1 large onion (200g), sliced finely
2 cloves garlic, crushed
400g can tomatoes, drained, chopped
1 green chilli, chopped finely
½ teaspoon salt
½ teaspoon freshly ground black pepper
½ cup (125ml) chicken stock

1 Slice aubergines into 1cm-thick rounds. Place rounds on paper towel, sprinkle lightly with cooking salt, then top with paper towel; smooth paper towel over rounds. Stand 20 minutes; discard paper towel. Rinse aubergine under cold water, pat dry with paper towel; chop aubergine slices into 1cm cubes.
2 Heat oil in large heavy-base saucepan; cook pork, in batches, until brown all over. Set aside.
3 Add onion, garlic and aubergine to same pan; cook for 10 minutes or until onion is beginning to brown and aubergine has absorbed most of the oil.
4 Add pork, tomato, chilli, salt, black pepper and stock; simmer, covered, stirring occasionally, 1 hour.
5 Serve with plain boiled rice and a crunchy mixed-leaf salad, if desired.

serves 4

caribbean pork roast

preparation time 15 minutes (plus marinating time)
cooking time 2 hours 30 minutes

2kg leg of pork, with rind
12 cloves
2 tablespoons dark rum
1 tablespoon dark brown sugar
2 teaspoons finely grated lime rind
⅓ cup (80ml) lime juice
½ teaspoon ground nutmeg
½ teaspoon ground coriander
½ teaspoon salt
1 tablespoon olive oil
1 cup (250ml) orange juice
1 tablespoon soy sauce

1 Score pork rind, right through to flesh. Press cloves deeply into score marks. Place pork in baking dish.
2 Combine rum, sugar, rind, lime juice, spices, salt and oil in small bowl. Pour rum mixture over pork, directing mixture into score marks, cover; refrigerate 3 hours, occasionally spooning marinade into score marks.
3 Preheat oven to moderate.
4 Roast pork, uncovered, in moderate oven 2 hours, basting occasionally.
5 Increase oven temperature to moderately hot; roast pork, uncovered, in moderately hot oven further 20 minutes. This will make the skin (crackling) crisper. Remove pork from dish; set aside in warm place.
6 Skim off any excess fat from pan juices in baking dish; discard fat. Add orange juice; mix well with pan juices. Pour juice mixture into small saucepan, add soy sauce, bring to a boil; boil, uncovered, until sauce has reduced by a third.
7 Remove crackling and carve pork; discard cloves. Serve pork with sauce and crackling, and a selection of vegetables, if desired.

serves 6

rum steaks

preparation time 10 minutes (plus marinating time)
cooking time 10 minutes

4 cloves garlic, crushed
1 teaspoon salt
½ teaspoon freshly ground black pepper
1 tablespoon dry red wine
4 thin rump steaks (800g)
50g butter
2 medium onions (300g),sliced thinly
2 tablespoons dark rum
1 tablespoon whole black peppercorns
½ cup (125ml) single cream

1 Combine garlic, salt, pepper and wine in small bowl.
Arrange steaks on a plate, spread wine mixture over top, cover;
refrigerate at least 1 hour.
2 Melt butter in medium heavy-based frying pan; sear steaks
over high heat, in batches, not more than 1 minute each side.
Set steaks aside in warm place.
3 Reduce heat to medium, add onion to same pan; cook until
onion is soft and beginning to brown.
4 Add rum and peppercorns; stir well. Reduce heat to low; add
cream, stirring. Bring sauce to boiling point; remove from heat.
5 Pour sauce over steaks to serve.

serves 4

FISH & SEAFOOD

There are so many different fish available in the Caribbean that a style of cooking has been developed that works with most varieties. In these recipes we have suggested a type of fish to use, but you should not feel inhibited about swapping salmon for cod, or halibut for plaice. Each variety of fish brings a different result when matched with the tropical ingredients.

trinidad fish bake

preparation time 10 minutes (plus marinating time)
cooking time 30 minutes

1 cup (280g) plain yogurt
1 tablespoon curry powder
1 tablespoon desiccated coconut
2 shallots, chopped finely
2 cloves garlic, crushed
1 tablespoon olive oil
½ teaspoon salt
½ teaspoon freshly ground black pepper
3 teaspoons finely grated lime rind
½ cup (125ml) lime juice
4 halibut steaks (700g)

1 Preheat oven to moderate.
2 Combine yogurt, curry powder, coconut, shallot, garlic, oil, salt, pepper, rind and juice in shallow baking dish. Add fish, spooning yogurt mixture over fish to coat. Cover; refrigerate at least 1 hour.
3 Bake fish, uncovered, in moderate oven 30 minutes, occasionally basting with marinade.
4 Serve with lime wedges, if desired.

serves 4

tip If you prefer, use cod steaks instead of halibut.

trout with mango and ginger

Although most Caribbean fish recipes use saltwater fish, some freshwater fish dishes are also popular. The vivid colour and wonderful taste of the mango, plus the delicate flavour of tarragon, make this a memorable dish.

preparation time 20 minutes
cooking time 45 minutes

2 tablespoons plain flour
½ teaspoon salt
½ teaspoon freshly ground black pepper
4 small trout (about 1.5kg), cleaned and scaled
2 medium mangoes (860g), stone removed, chopped coarsely
3 cloves garlic, crushed
1 tablespoon finely chopped fresh tarragon
1 medium onion (150g), chopped finely
2 medium tomatoes (380g), chopped finely
2 tablespoons grated fresh ginger
1 teaspoon light brown sugar
1 cup (250ml) fish stock
50g butter
2 spring onions, cut into long strips

1 Combine flour, salt and pepper on a plate. Toss fish in seasoned flour, shake off excess.
2 Blend or process mango, garlic, tarragon, onion, tomato, ginger, sugar and stock until smooth; set aside.
3 Melt butter in large heavy-based frying pan; cook fish, in batches, occasionally pressing fish into pan with flat side of a fish-slice, 6 minutes each side or until well browned all over. Set aside in warm place.
4 Add blended sauce to same pan, stir into pan juices. Bring to a boil; simmer, uncovered, 2 minutes, then return fish to pan. Spoon sauce over fish, cover; simmer gently for 15 minutes, turning fish once.
5 Serve fish topped with sauce and spring onion.

serves 4

tip If you prefer, use 2 teaspoons dried tarragon in place of the fresh tarragon.

pepper fish

preparation time 15 minutes
cooking time 25 minutes

2 tablespoons plain flour
½ teaspoon salt
¼ teaspoon freshly ground black
    pepper
4 plaice fillets (700g)
50g butter
1 large onion (200g), sliced finely
2 cloves garlic, crushed
2 medium red peppers (400g), cut
    into 1cm strips
½ cup (125ml) dry white wine
5 medium tomatoes (1kg), peeled,
    deseeded, chopped finely
4 spring onions, chopped finely

1 Combine flour, salt and black pepper in medium shallow dish. Toss fish in seasoned flour, shake off excess.
2 Melt butter in large frying pan; cook fish, in batches, 2 minutes each side or until golden brown. Set aside.
3 Add onion, garlic and pepper to same pan; cook until onion is soft.
4 Add wine and tomato, bring to a boil; return fish to pan, covering it with vegetables and juices. Cover; simmer 10 minutes.
5 Serve sprinkled with spring onion.

serves 4

baked salmon steaks

preparation time 10 minutes
cooking time 10 minutes
(plus standing time)

2 tablespoons fresh lime juice
2 cloves garlic, crushed
2 teaspoons sweet chilli sauce
2 tablespoons olive oil
4 salmon steaks (700g)
1 lime, cut into eight thin slices

1 Preheat oven to moderate.
2 Combine juice, garlic, sauce and oil in small bowl; whisk until blended.
3 Lightly oil large piece of foil, place on oven tray. Place fish on foil, turn up edges of foil; pour lime juice mixture over fish.
4 Place two slices of lime on each fish steak. Place another sheet of foil over top; fold foil edges to seal tightly.
5 Bake fish in moderate oven for 10 minutes; stand 5 minutes before opening foil and serving.

serves 4

tip Serve with thin barbecued slices of sweet potato and a crispy green salad.

bream with tomato coriander salsa

preparation time 25 minutes
cooking time 30 minutes

4 large tomatoes (1kg), peeled, deseeded, chopped finely
1 green chilli, chopped finely
1 small red onion (100g), chopped finely
2 tablespoons lime juice
3 tablespoons finely chopped fresh coriander leaves
salt, to taste
pepper, to taste
4 medium potatoes (800g), peeled, cut into even-sized pieces
100g butter
4 bream fillets (about 750g)
1 teaspoon sweet paprika

1 Combine tomato, chilli, onion, juice, coriander, salt and pepper in large bowl; set aside.
2 Place potato in large saucepan of cold water with 1 teaspoon salt. Bring to a boil, reduce heat; simmer, uncovered, 15-20 minutes or until potato is tender.
3 Meanwhile, melt half of the butter in grill pan. Add fish; turn so that fillets are coated in melted butter on both sides. Sprinkle fish with a little extra salt and pepper; cook, turning once, 6 minutes or until lightly browned all over and cooked through.
4 Drain potatoes; mash with remaining butter and paprika. Add a little milk if you prefer a moister mash.
5 Serve each fillet on a bed of mashed potato with tomato coriander salsa.

serves 4

crab gumbo

preparation time 20 minutes
cooking time 20 minutes

400g white cabbage, chopped coarsely
400g spinach leaves, stems removed
200g watercress
1 cup fresh flat-leaf parsley leaves
50g butter
2 medium onions (300g),chopped finely
2 medium tomatoes (380g), chopped coarsely
1 fresh red chilli, chopped finely
1 teaspoon fresh thyme leaves
1 teaspoon finely chopped fresh marjoram
1 teaspoon ground allspice
½ teaspoon salt
½ teaspoon freshly ground black pepper
400g fresh crab meat
100g radishes, sliced thinly

1 Place cabbage, spinach, watercress and parsley in large saucepan with just enough water to cover. Bring to a boil; simmer, uncovered, 1 minute. Drain vegetables; reserve liquid. Chop vegetables finely.
2 Melt butter in large heavy-based saucepan; cook onion, stirring, until lightly browned. Add chopped vegetables, tomato, chilli, thyme, marjoram, allspice, salt and black pepper; stir well. Add 1 cup of the reserved vegetable liquid, bring to a boil; simmer, uncovered, 5 minutes or until liquid has almost evaporated.
3 Add crab meat and radish; stir until heated through.
4 Serve crab gumbo with boiled rice, if desired.

serves 4

tip If you prefer, use ½ teaspoon dried thyme and ½ teaspoon dried marjoram in place of fresh thyme and fresh marjoram. Frozen or tinned crab meat can be used instead of fresh crab meat.

SALSAS & SIDES

The word 'salsa' refers to tangy combinations of sweet and savoury fruit and vegetables that accompany a main meal. Other traditional Caribbean sides include potatoes – sweet or otherwise – rice, okra, aubergine and a variety of legumes such as pigeon peas, black-eye beans, haricot beans and red kidney beans.

hoppin' john

preparation time 15 minutes
cooking time 35 minutes

3 cups (750ml) chicken stock
1 large tomato (250g), chopped coarsely
⅓ cup finely chopped spring onions
1 green chilli, deseeded, chopped finely
2 teaspoons fresh thyme leaves
1 bay leaf
½ teaspoon saffron threads
12 whole black peppercorns
1¼ cups (250g) white long-grain rice
4 rashers thick-cut back bacon, cut into large pieces
450g can black-eye beans, drained
salt, to taste

1 Bring stock to a boil in large saucepan, add tomato, onion, chilli, thyme, bay leaf, saffron and peppercorns; boil, uncovered, 2 minutes. Add rice; simmer, uncovered, stirring occasionally, 15 minutes. If necessary, add a little water to prevent rice from drying out.
2 Meanwhile, cook bacon in medium non-stick frying pan until cooked through, but not crisp.
3 Stir bacon and beans into rice mixture; simmer, uncovered, stirring occasionally, 10 minutes or until rice is cooked and liquid is absorbed.
4 Discard bay leaf; add salt before serving.

serves 4

lentil salsa

preparation time 15 minutes
cooking time 35 minutes

½ cup (100g) green lentils
1 cup (250ml) cold water
2 tablespoons finely chopped fresh
    coriander leaves
2 large tomatoes (500g), peeled,
    deseeded, cut into 1cm pieces
½ medium red onion (85g),
    chopped finely
1 fresh red chilli, deseeded,
    chopped finely
2 tablespoons lime juice
2 tablespoons olive oil
salt, to taste
freshly ground black pepper, to taste

1 Rinse lentils under cold water.
Place in medium saucepan with the
water, bring to a boil. Cover, reduce
heat; simmer 30 minutes or until lentils
are just tender.
2 Rinse lentils under cold water;
drain. Place lentils in medium bowl,
add remaining ingredients; stir well.
Cover; refrigerate until cold.
3 Serve salsa with fish or chicken,
if desired.

serves 4

hot barbecue salsa

preparation time 15 minutes
cooking time 15 minutes

1 tablespoon olive oil
1 medium onion (150g), chopped
    coarsely
2 cloves garlic, crushed
2 green chillies, deseeded, chopped
    finely
400g can tomatoes, drained,
    deseeded, chopped
1 tablespoon finely chopped fresh
    flat-leaf parsley
1 teaspoon hot paprika
½ teaspoon salt
½ teaspoon freshly ground black
    pepper

1 Heat oil in medium saucepan; cook
onion and garlic until onion is soft.
2 Add remaining ingredients to pan;
simmer, uncovered, 10 minutes.
3 Serve warm salsa with barbecued
beef, lamb or chicken, if desired.

serves 4

*clockwise from top left: lentil
salsa, sweet and sour salad,
hot barbecue salsa*

sweet and sour salad

preparation time 15 minutes

2 medium oranges (480g)
2 tablespoons plain yogurt
2 tablespoons lime juice
300g shredded white cabbage
1 medium apple (150g), grated
  coarsely
½ cucumber (130g), sliced finely
2 medium tomatoes (380g),
  chopped coarsely

1 Peel and thinly slice oranges; cut slices into quarters.
2 Combine yogurt and juice in small bowl or jug; stir until smooth.
3 Combine orange with remaining ingredients in large bowl; drizzle with yogurt mixture, toss to combine.

serves 6

mango salsa

preparation time 20 minutes

1 medium mango (430g), stone removed, chopped finely
1 medium red onion (170g), chopped finely
1 medium red pepper (200g), chopped finely
1 tablespoon finely chopped fresh marjoram
½ teaspoon ground ginger
1 tablespoon olive oil

1 Combine ingredients in medium bowl, cover; refrigerate until cold.
2 Serve salsa with any barbecued dish.

serves 4

sweet potato stir

preparation time 10 minutes
cooking time 30 minutes

2 small sweet potatoes (500g),
  cut into 2cm pieces
1 teaspoon salt
2 tablespoons olive oil
1 large onion (200g), chopped
  coarsely
2 cloves garlic, sliced finely
1 teaspoon ground cumin
450g can red kidney beans,
  drained
1 teaspoon finely grated lime rind
2 tablespoons lime juice
2 tablespoons finely chopped
  fresh coriander leaves

1 Place potato and salt in large saucepan of cold water. Bring to a boil, reduce heat; simmer, uncovered, until potato is just tender, drain. Do not overcook, or potato will become mushy when fried.
2 Heat oil in large frying pan, add potato; cook 5 minutes or until potato is beginning to brown. Add onion and garlic; cook, using a fish-slice to turn potato without breaking, until onion is beginning to brown.
3 Add cumin, beans, rind and juice; cook until beans are heated through.
4 Stir coriander through mixture just before serving.

serves 4

barbados cou-cou

Traditional cou-cou is made with cornmeal. We have substituted the more readily available polenta, made from ground maize, which gives the same result.

preparation time 5 minutes
cooking time 35 minutes

400g okra, trimmed, sliced thickly
1 teaspoon salt
3 cups (750ml) cold water
¾ cup (180ml) coconut milk
1½ cups (250g) polenta
30g butter
½ teaspoon freshly ground black
   pepper

1 Place okra in large saucepan with salt and the water. Bring to a boil, reduce heat; simmer, uncovered, about 10 minutes. Drain okra; reserve cooking liquid.
2 Pour coconut milk and ½ cup (125ml) of the reserved cooking liquid into large saucepan; bring to a boil. Add okra, then gradually add polenta, beating vigorously. If necessary, add more reserved cooking liquid to keep the polenta moist but not runny; cook, stirring constantly so polenta doesn't stick to pan, 5 minutes. Cover; cook 10 minutes, stirring occasionally.
3 To serve, spread cou-cou with butter; sprinkle with pepper.

serves 4

green papaya salsa

preparation time 20 minutes

2 tablespoons lime juice
2 teaspoons dark brown sugar
1 teaspoon finely grated lime rind
1 medium green papaya (1kg), deseeded, chopped finely
2 tablespoons finely chopped fresh coriander leaves
1 fresh red chilli, deseeded, chopped finely
1 medium red onion (170g), chopped finely
1 tablespoon olive oil

1 Place juice in large bowl, add sugar; stir until sugar is dissolved. Add remaining ingredients; stir well. Cover; refrigerate until cold.
2 Serve salsa with grilled fish or barbecued chicken, if desired.

serves 8

glossary

allspice also known as pimento or jamaican pepper; available whole or ground.

angostura aromatic bitters based on rum and infused with bitter aromatic bark, herbs and spices.

aniseed also called anise; the licorice-flavoured seeds of the anise plant.

banana, green an ordinary banana that has been picked before it is fully ripe.

beans

black-eye also known as black-eyed peas; small beige legumes with black circular eyes. Available dried or tinned.

red kidney pink to maroon beans with a floury texture and fairly sweet flavour; sold dried or tinned.

bouquet garni a combination of thyme, parsley and a bay leaf, tied together with kitchen string or placed in a muslin bag; it is usually removed before serving.

cayenne pepper hot spice made from dried ground pods of chillies.

chickpeas also called garbanzos or channa; irregularly round, sandy-coloured legumes used extensively in Caribbean, Mediterranean and Middle-Eastern cooking.

chilli available in many different types and sizes. Use rubber gloves when deseeding and chopping fresh chilli, as they can burn your skin. Removing seeds and membranes reduces the heat level.

powder made from ground chilli; use as a substitute for fresh chilli peppers in the proportion of ½ teaspoon ground chilli powder to one medium chopped fresh chilli pepper.

sauce we used a hot Chinese variety made of chilli peppers, salt and vinegar; use sparingly, increasing amounts to taste.

coconut

cream available in tins and cartons; as a rule, proportions are two parts coconut to one part water.

desiccated unsweetened, concentrated, dried, shredded coconut flesh.

milk pure, unsweetened coconut milk available in tins and cartons.

coriander also known as cilantro or Chinese parsley; a bright-green leafy herb with a pungent flavour.

curaçao orange-flavoured liqueur.

curry powder mixture of ground coriander, chilli peppers, cumin, fennel, cinnamon, fenugreek and turmeric in varying proportions.

garam masala a spice mixture consisting of varying combinations of cardamom, cinnamon, cloves, cumin, coriander and fennel roasted and ground.

ginger root

fresh also known as green ginger; the thick gnarled root of a tropical plant. Peel the outside skin and grate, chop or slice as required.

ground also called powdered ginger; no substitute for fresh ginger root.

green peppercorns soft, unripe berries of the pepper plant usually sold in brine.

mango a round fruit about the size of a large pear, with green skin turning orange-yellow when ripe; if fresh mangoes are not available, use tinned.

chutney a mild, sweet chutney made from mangoes and spices.

milk

condensed canned milk product with more than half the water content removed and sugar added to the milk that remains.

evaporated unsweetened canned milk from which water has been extracted by evaporation.

mustard

french a smooth, mild mustard with a sweet-sour taste.

wholegrain flavoursome, coarse-grained, fairly hot mustard containing white wine.

nutmeg the dried nut of an evergreen tree; available whole or in ground form.

okra also known as gumbo or lady's fingers; a green, ridged, oblong pod with a furry skin used to thicken stews. Rinse and cut off capped end close to stalk.

olive oil made from the pressing of tree-ripened olives. Extra virgin and virgin olive oil are the highest quality, obtained from the first pressings of the olives.

paprika ground dried red pepper, available sweet or hot.

papaya also known as pawpaw or papaw; large, pear-shaped red-orange tropical fruit. Sometimes used unripe (green) in cooking.

polenta a flour-like cereal made of ground corn (maize).

rum liquor made from fermented sugarcane; dark and light varieties are available.

saffron the stigma of a member of the crocus family; available in strands or ground form. Imparts a yellow-orange colour to food once infused. Quality varies greatly, with the best being the most expensive spice in the world. Should be stored in the freezer.

shallots small, elongated, brown-skinned members of the onion family.

soy sauce made from fermented soy beans. Several variations are available.

sweet chilli sauce a fairly mild, but spicy sauce made from red chilli peppers, sugar, garlic and vinegar.

sweet potato fleshy root vegetable; available with red or white flesh.

worcestershire sauce a thin, dark-brown, spicy sauce used as seasoning for meat and gravies, and as a condiment.

conversion charts

MEASURES

The cup and spoon measurements used in this book are metric: one measuring cup holds approximately 250ml; one metric tablespoon holds 20ml; one metric teaspoon holds 5ml.

All cup and spoon measurements are level.

The most accurate way of measuring dry ingredients is to weigh them. When measuring liquids, use a clear glass or plastic jug with metric markings.

We use large eggs with an average weight of 60g.

warning This book may contain recipes for dishes made with raw or lightly cooked eggs. These should be avoided by vulnerable people such as pregnant and nursing mothers, invalids, the elderly, babies and young children.

DRY MEASURES

METRIC	IMPERIAL
15g	½oz
30g	1oz
60g	2oz
90g	3oz
125g	4oz (¼lb)
155g	5oz
185g	6oz
220g	7oz
250g	8oz (½lb)
280g	9oz
315g	10oz
345g	11oz
375g	12oz (¾lb)
410g	13oz
440g	14oz
470g	15oz
500g	16oz (1lb)
750g	24oz (1½lb)
1kg	32oz (2lb)

LIQUID MEASURES

METRIC	IMPERIAL
30ml	1 fl oz
60ml	2 fl oz
100ml	3 fl oz
125ml	4 fl oz
150ml	5 fl oz (¼ pint/1 gill)
190ml	6 fl oz
250ml	8 fl oz
300ml	10 fl oz (½ pint)
500ml	16 fl oz
600ml	20 fl oz (1 pint)
1000ml (1 litre)	1¾ pints

LENGTH MEASURES

METRIC	IMPERIAL
3mm	⅛in
6mm	¼in
1cm	½in
2cm	¾in
2.5cm	1in
5cm	2in
6cm	2½in
8cm	3in
10cm	4in
13cm	5in
15cm	6in
18cm	7in
20cm	8in
23cm	9in
25cm	10in
28cm	11in
30cm	12in (1ft)

OVEN TEMPERATURES

These oven temperatures are only a guide for conventional ovens.
For fan-assisted ovens, check the manufacturer's manual.

	°C (CELSIUS)	°F (FAHRENHEIT)	GAS MARK
Very low	120	250	½
Low	150	275–300	1–2
Moderately low	160	325	3
Moderate	180	350–375	4–5
Moderately hot	200	400	6
Hot	220	425–450	7–8
Very hot	240	475	9

index